Bending Light with Bare Hands

A Journal of Poems

The poems in David B. Prather's second full-length collection, *Bending Light with Bare Hands*, are woven from thunderstorms, omens, insomnia—even the telltale signs of a body in slow decline. With language that manages the oxymoronic feat of being both concise and lavish, the poet takes an unflinching look at subjects that include depression, loneliness, and the longing to hold on to memories, even while acknowledging their unreliable nature. If Prather puts his faith in anything, it is in the gods of this world, who inhabit the bodies of hummingbirds, katydids, bats, and mockingbirds, who weave their beds with bindweed and ivy, and write in the luminescent script of fireflies, constellations, and even headlights. This collection quickly and unrelentingly distinguishes itself, elevating the quotidian into meditations on love, mortality, and mental health. Prather is a poet who has hit his stride. I have seldom been more pleased to lend my name to a book's cover.

—Frank Paino
author of *Obscura*

Written throughout the pandemic, this essential journal of poems is an intimate account of restless days spent attempting hope on the south side of Parkersburg, West Virginia. A sense of impending doom, rendered though it is with wonder, wit, and wounded amusement, lingers long after lockdown. "Every little ache in the body/ becomes a symptom" that cannot be ignored; every little sliver of light seems a reprieve, yet it remains "hard not to believe we/ are being punished." In a world that all too often "refuses to give us/ what we need," Prather masterfully melds myth and memory, fire-and-brimstone brow-beatings, folklore, flawed family legacies, and the bittersweet lessons of a lifetime into luminous verse that verges on salvation.

—Randi Ward
author of *Whipstitches*

Bending Light with Bare Hands, David B. Prather's sophomore collection, illuminates in a world of shadows. Moving seamlessly from the everyday to the deepest questions of our time, Prather is as comfortable growing heirloom tomatoes and cooking his grandmother's vegetable soup as he is grappling with dark matter and the injustices of species extinction. "If I had wings, I would be a nightbird, and I would sing to bring down the stars" he writes. No need for such dramatic transformation—these poems sing and leave us basking in their glow.

—Denton Loving
author of *Tamp*

Bending Light with Bare Hands

A Journal of Poems

by

David B. Prather

Bending Light with Bare Hands

©2025 by David B. Prather

Fernwood Press
Newberg, Oregon
www.fernwoodpress.com

All rights reserved. No part may be reproduced
for any commercial purpose by any method without
permission in writing from the copyright holder.

Printed in the United States of America

Cover and page design: Mareesa Fawver Moss
Cover art: Dynamic Wang

ISBN 978-1-59498-155-5

for my parents

With thanks to the writers who helped me with their insights on much of this manuscript: Wilma Acree, Kari Gunter-Seymour, Hayley Haugen, Sean Kelbley, Stephanie Kendrick, and Sherrell Wigal. These poets inspire me with their friendship and their talents.

Contents

Fear of Darkness 12
186,000 Miles Per Second 14
Freeze Warning 15
Germination 17
Maintenance 18
Apiary 20
Dental Work 21
Memorial Day 23
One Month Until Summer 25
A Drop in Barometric Pressure 27
Lightning 29
Electrical Grid 31
Shopping for My Grandmother During a Pandemic 33
Afternoon Meditation 35
Astigmatism 37
All I Talk About Is the Weather 39
Storm upon Us 41
Another Day of Rain 43
Learning to Play Piano 45
After Considering Not Planting a Garden 47
Father's Day 49
Heritage 51

Maternal	53
Black-and-White Photos	54
Cutting My Hair	55
Given Warning	57
Such a Day as Today	59
Incident at Night	60
Half the Year Gone	62
Even If It Takes All Night	64
Mapping Stars in City Light	66
Spending the Night Alone	68
What Keeps Me Up at Night	70
Sleepless	72
The Light at Night	74
Emblematic	76
Funeral Planning	78
Foresight	80
By Another Name	83
Ever Changing	84
Desire	86
Entomology	87
Off the Earth	89
Neighbors	91
Cut Glass Candy Dish	93
Impossible Solitude	95
Mythology	96
Pandemic	98
Rain Crow	99
Where There is Forgiveness	101
Those Who Stay Behind	103
Apocalypse	105
Biography	107
Acknowledgments	109
Title Index	111
First Line Index	115

God is an abstract noun.

—Charles Wright
from *A Journal of English Days*

Fear of Darkness

Lately, I begin to wonder how long it'll be
                          before my eyes
cloud over, force me to speak only of storms
                          and shadows.
Today, I see a pale mist where there is none,
                          a matter of summer
sunlight and the failure of my retina. My mother
                          tells me what
I already know, that I shouldn't ignore this.
                          But it has always
been her job to state the obvious. She tells me
                          she'll never see
a sequoia, never stand beside those fabled trees.
                          Fabled to her,
like the dodo, the Franklin tree, or any of the
                          ninety-nine percent
of all species ever to have failed to survive
                          this world.
If someone asks how I am, I say *I'm just*
                          surviving,
which is more than I can say for so many
                          others. At dusk,
every light is a supernova, oncoming traffic,
                          streetlights,
the glowing signs of businesses closed
                          for the night.
But I keep finding my way home. It's all a matter
                          of reflex, anyway,
kind of how I wander the house in the morning,
                          eyelids shut,
kitchen, coffee, living room, television, voices.
                          My mother
used to yell for me to wake when a whisper would
                          startle me.

Once, I dreamed a monster breaking my window,
                              dragging me
from my car. I woke seated at the edge of my bed,
                              transported from
one reality to another, perhaps dimensional drift,
                              sliding around,
proving string theory. It's a fact the eye is useless
                              without light,
which is not a god. And yet I can be blinded,
                              refraction,
reflection, glare, seeing haloes around every
                              illumination.
I'm sure they can't all be angels.

186,000 Miles Per Second

Running late again, I meant to be
                elsewhere an hour ago, a lifetime ago.
     I'm prone to exaggeration. I rush around,
misplace my keys, forget my wallet,
                lock the door, then remember the one thing
         I need most. I need the curtains over
the kitchen window to gap and let in
          a sliver of morning. I need moonlight
     in my bedroom to check my breathing,
to put its hand on my forehead, feel
           for fever. I need the amber illumination
     of streetlights to make me reconsider
what I've left undone. The world is a clock
           running backwards. No wonder
     I'm always speeding through town,
swerving in and out of traffic, a comet
           careening through the solar system.
    This is the fate of heavenly bodies,
a matter of constant motion, always
          in a hurry, a tizzy, going full tilt
       among the stars. I have no heavenly
traits. I've heard water drains counter-
          clockwise in the southern hemisphere,
     but my friends balk at the thought,
as though I made it up, as though I were
          trying to bend light with my bare hands.
    And I want to tell them, in a way, I can.
So can they. But no one thinks in terms
          of photons, which have energy,
     but no mass. If only I could move that fast,
I could be everywhere, omnipresent, except
           in those places where whippoorwills sing.
    For this, I will close my eyes. For this,
I can count the hours as if they were stars.

Freeze Warning

Three ghostly figures stand motionless
in the neighbor's lawn, sheets draped over saplings.

I am startled. It is late, and night spreads

a cold blanket. I admit I took a sudden
breath, sure that these were people wandering

in the chill. We are conditioned to be scared,

and I've seen too many movies
where the most dangerous patients roam free

to harm those of us who haven't heard

the warnings, the sirens. Searchlights
fall on nothing but a fine mist freezing

every tenderness. Tonight, the moon

gathers close, reveals itself completely
as a harbinger of long swaths of arctic air.

Everyone is caught off guard. This late

in the year we shiver when all we want
is to remove all these layers of clothing,

burn our skin under promiscuous sunlight.

It touches the forehead with fever,
the back of the thigh with passion.

How can it be? We can hardly wait

to melt ice crystals in our veins.
I wonder if we haven't brought this

upon ourselves. In orchards, smudge pots

are lit, burn fierce as stars. Trash fires
crackle and shush. People reach

their hands close to the flame as ashes

rise past their phantom faces.
Forecasters keep telling us to cover

our vulnerable plants. But I would like to hear

more about the future. Will I need to worry
about the end of the world? Will it come

as a meteor or a virus? A war? An invasion

of extraterrestrial monsters unlike anything
I've yet to imagine? I've already seen movement

across the street, those specters touched

by a bone-chilling breeze. It gets into the marrow,
freezes our blood as we sleep.

Germination

My father brings me seeds he ordered from a catalog,
    says, *Here's those heirloom tomatoes
you like so much.* But I know he wouldn't buy them
    unless he wanted them. I think
he's forgotten the trouble I've had with seedlings,
    not enough natural light in the house,
the tender plants stretching themselves thin. I tell
    my father that I'll do what I can,
explain again I have too little light. Less than half
    survive to be carried outside
in better weather. Freeze advisories keep me
    pinning curtain panels to the wisteria,
but the cold air cannot be stopped, all the buds
    susceptible. I should go to the nursery
to replace what has been lost. I should lie about
    these spindly stems and withered
leaves. Now there's nothing but rain, and the soil
    is too wet. And I don't know
what my father expects. The earth must be turned,
    made ready. Last autumn, squirrels
left acorns in the fallow ground. Now, saplings take
    root, these cast-off bits of life rising
toward the sun, so hardy, so resilient. I am amazed
    at all the things my body cannot do,
like a dandelion full of such wonderful thoughts
    they drift away with the wind.
The season moves on. Soon it will be too late
    to anticipate any harvest. Now,
I understand how people go hungry, how sometimes
    the world refuses to give us
what we need. Which is different for us all. Sometimes
    an ocean trench. Sometimes arctic ice.
Sometimes all I need is some arable land, a few uncloudy
    days, and a handful of seeds. Sometimes
I just need my father to tell me even this ground is good.

Maintenance

                Aluminum siding needs painted
to cover those faint gray patches only I can see.
          And the porch needs a new coat
of blue to hide the wear of weather and footsteps.
        I know two places where shingles
let a hard rain in, shirking their duty, admitting
              defeat. The only soul to inhabit
this house, I know how quiet means listening,
           for the hum of traffic, for the
chit chat of finches, for the startled voices
                of neighbors to trouble me
through these thin walls. The hardwood floors
                grow weak in a few spots, but
they are level. There's a spot at the front
              door that warns any haunts
I'm home. I couldn't sneak out if I wanted,
               all the hinges hoarse with my
going and coming back. I always come back.
            Some of the windows no longer
open, and a few screens have been missing so long
               there isn't even a memory
they ever existed. In the basement, there are names
                carved into wooden beams,
Joey and Susan, children or lovers, I can't say, but
                this is evidence, nonetheless,
of lives lived long before I spoke my first word,
                which my mother never
told me, never wrote down. As far as I know,
             I sprang from the timbers
of this house, my great grandmother's before me,
               her shelf paper under my dishes
and glasses, her recipes unused in the pantry
                next to olive oil and pancake mix,
her tarnished scissors with a broken tip
             holding her fingerprints

where they want to be held. I've changed the locks
    because I'm afraid
someone from the past might still have a key.
    I have a bowl full of keys
that have forgotten their purpose. The garden hose
    hanging over a patch
of spearmint still drips no matter how tightly
    the faucet is turned.

Apiary

                      Purplish blooms, my blazing stars
come back stronger every year, massaged by pollinators.
                      But not today. I haven't seen any
honeybees take their frenzied turns. A cold, wet spring,
                      and a burning start to summer,
I'm afraid the worker bees are gone, their queens curled
                      into apostrophes in their hives.
I even let white clover spread out through my lawn, these
                      blossoms my attempt at hope.
Which is something I had as a barefoot child, until one
                      careless step, and I was stung,
my foot swollen, unable to wear a shoe for a week. But
                      this wasn't my only lesson in pain.
There were sweat bees, bumblebees, yellow jackets,
                      hornets. There were wasps that
built their paper houses in my open windows during
                      the sweltering ages of childhood
when all we had was breezes and fans. I don't walk
                      barefoot across the lawn anymore.
I don't bend my elbows or knees without checking for
                      some sign of life. I don't sit at
old school bus stops on rainy mornings to learn this is shelter
                      for carpenter bees, mud daubers,
deer flies, red bugs. They write their own apocrypha,
                      their own explanations of the gods
pulled from flowers and dew. I've never been so worried
                      about the end of the world as I am
right now. Yes, there were warnings, there were signs.
                      I should have listened to the wisdom
of my grandparents who knew how to read the turnings
                      of leaves, the songs of birds. Which,
I just realized, I don't hear today. When the weather is hot,
                      there are flashes in the sky
my grandmother calls heat lightning. She says it doesn't
                      mean rain. It means
the devil is loose in the world, and he's near.

Dental Work

Sometimes mistaken for a flying insect,
   the Bee Hummingbird is the smallest
bird in the world. It's eggs are smaller
   than the tooth I lost years ago to bad
genes, which also gave me a curved
   spine and acid reflux. I could hold
an aviary of these birds in my mouth,
   their pinpoint hearts beating so
furiously, I'd feel it as a buzzing in
   my nerves. My father lost a tooth
before I was born, right in front, and
   he could flip out the false one to
tease me with that gap, that emptiness
   in his smile. And there's always been
a space between my mother's
   central incisors. I wonder now if the
young of the Bee Hummingbird has
   an egg tooth to escape its coffee-
bean-sized shell. The predators
   for such a diminutive creature
must be many—hornets, wasps,
   spiders, other bigger birds. I think
of my own predators, people who
   would do me harm, who would bare
their toothy smiles. I think of
   elephants and walruses, of warthogs
and narwhals, their entire lives defined
   by molar modification, which I phrase
for the sound. Once, perhaps, even
   I was the size of a tooth, or, that is,
the potential of me in the nest of
   the womb. I could have grown wings.
I could have sprouted iridescent feathers.

   I could have suckled the sweet nectar
of subtropical flowers brushed gently
   by cool trade winds. When I bare
my teeth, I know what I have lost.

Memorial Day

My sister and I never knew the dead,

every year those names repeated
to try to make us remember.

But without faces, without the sounds

of their voices, we only knew them
as stone markers, days and years

before we were born. Too young

to understand reverence, we were
cautioned not to step on the graves,

so we made respect a game,

as though setting foot upon a plot
was the same as jumping on our beds.

We'd been told we could break

our necks. And we knew this was true,
we'd heard stories of a long-gone cousin

who caught his foot in covers, lost

his balance, snapped his spine
against a wall. We'd never questioned

the truth, or considered the wisdom of God.

We carried fake flowers to graves.
We were even allowed to push

those wire stems into hallowed ground.
On some of the markers, there were crosses.

On others, angels.

Each cemetery was a chance for reunion,
friends and family gathered in the shade

of a butternut tree while a hot breeze

grabbed at shirtsleeves and pant legs.
We made a game of this, too,

trying to name the ghosts risen

to get our attention. We gave them
words, made them say things like

The treasure is buried under the forsythia,

or *Our fathers were never who we thought,*
or, *Yes, Heaven is more than we*

could ever dream, even as we lay in our beds,

our bodies so still, our breath so slow
it had to be checked throughout the night.

One Month Until Summer

A skunk has moved into the area, rummaging
    through all the shadowy places we've created,

a pile of brush, a crawl space, but more likely
    she's dug a den beneath the concrete pad

between my house and the neighbor's. When
    I pull my car in later than I should be getting

home, I can tell she's there, her musk lingering
    in my breezeway. I don't like to say she is

unwanted, but I'm not sure I can last through
    the birth and nurturing of kits. And I've only

learned that a group of skunks is called a *surfeit*,
    which means an excessive amount. Sometimes,

I remind myself of definitions to make a word
    stick to all those unused portions of my brain.

In which case, I offer the word *mephitis*,
    a noxious vapor. The world heads for the murkiest

moment of night, and air pauses in its travels.
    None of the evening voices have returned yet,

crickets not quite ready for love, nocturnal
    birds unwilling to start their songs. In the past

couple of years, a mockingbird has practiced
    his plagiarism in the dark branches of wisteria,

which happens to be too close to my bedroom
    window. I suppose I should be thankful

any living thing would come near, make
    themselves blessings or omens that I will

interpret only after time has proven signs
   one way or the other. For now, I'll keep

the windows closed and wait for morning
   to come in on a breeze to clear the stale air

away from the corners of this house where
   I've listened all night for an old, familiar tune.

A Drop in Barometric Pressure

A dull headache for two days is one of my signs
                for an oncoming storm,
a downpour. My grandmother is a weather witch,

                    which may be why I feel
changes in the sky. I'm no meteorologist, no
                    climatologist. I don't study

isobars or oscillation indices. I couldn't even
              explain what they are.
The women in my family have an emotional link

                to clouds and lightning.
In some drought-ridden areas, towns suffered
                the scams of rainmakers

who said they could coax water from the firmament
                with fervent prayers.
They knew how to appeal to God. Which is nothing

             like that Kate Bush video
for her song, "Cloudbusting," where Donald Sutherland
                invents a machine

to wring rain from ungiving clouds. This is not
              the same as seeding them
with chemicals to make the water heavy, to make

              its only desire a yearning
to fall. As though rain could feel anything, like me,
                caught in a torrent,

standing in a storefront alcove, my clothes clinging
              to my body, the intimacy
of a sudden storm. I've seen people dance for rain,

                    pound the earth
with rhythmic steps, cleanse the ground of evil
                    spirits who would rather

parch and burn. And now I really want to listen to
                    that song, "Cloudbusting,"
to see if it could release the pressure, to thunder down

                    the rainfall. If only
I had that kind of power, to be able to reach that high,
                    pull down those blessings.

Lightning

Judging by the clouds this morning, unmoved,
with tatters of sunlight, no one will remember
      the gloam. Last night,
lightning raced with thoughts, which is only
one of the reasons I don't sleep. *Can't.*
                      I mean I *can't* sleep.
Meaning inability, not willfulness. I think of
Ben Franklin's kite, the myth that he was struck.
      I worry about the keys
in my pocket, all those stories of people touched
by light, their own keys melted, trying to become
                  one with the body
that carries them. Irrational, I know, but I
sometimes believe I am a piece of fulgurite,
      a body fused together
by all that energy, bits and pieces of the earth
turned to a glassy form. My father used to
                  make glass at a factory
along the Little Kanawha River where there was
once a deposit of silica sand. I have no idea
      how it got there. Maybe
millions of years of weather, wind and rain,
hail and flood. My father hates impurities.
                In glass, flaws and bubbles.
Years ago, I touched a hot wire, electricity
snaked up my arm, near my heart. Which
      is a kiln, and imperfect.
I have a vase I prize for its stretch marks, those
pockets of air showing how the glass was
                  pulled into body, shoulder,
neck, and flare. My anger flares, but not today.
I shouldn't have stood outside where the sky yelled
      like a father vexed

by his son. We know there is love. Sometimes
a fulmination. But always a thunderbolt, something
                    so powerful
it can only emanate from the heavens.

Electrical Grid

Pigeons perch on power lines for two days
        in front of my house, which may not mean
anything to passersby, but to me it's an omen.
        The transformer is two doors down on a pole

that leans away from the street, and, I think,
        will one day break toward the houses it
feeds. I've seen a transformer blow, scatter
        sparks to a stormy afternoon, leave entire

neighborhoods in shadows and darkness.
        I wonder if these pigeons feel the surge of
energy in their feet as they grip the wire,
        if it pulses through their bodies. Years ago,

I can't remember how many, I touched
        an exposed, live outlet and felt the snakes
of electricity race for my heart. My hand
        felt that bite for an hour after. I wish

I knew the mythology of pigeons, what
        it means when they all face west as though
waiting to watch the sun set, when I know
        they are waiting for something else. I don't

know how I know. I just do. Perhaps there
        is a new pantheon of gods trembling at the
horizon, ready for that moment when people
        start to believe in something else, something

that will change the world. I know that kind
        of excitement. I remember, as a child, how
I couldn't sleep because tomorrow was a
        journey to somewhere I'd never been, an

amusement park, a spot on the river to fish
          and waste an afternoon, a walk in the woods
with no destination. Back then, I couldn't
          identify birds by their songs. But they

weren't singing to me. I see now the clouds
          are dancing. What music they must hear.

Shopping for My Grandmother During a Pandemic

            She tells me, *again*, that she won't
see the end of this sickness, this
                worldwide struggle. She has her own
worries—weight loss, fatigue, breath
                    no more than a gasp. On her list,
peanuts. She wants bags of legumes
                in their shells. For squirrels. She watches
them play in the driveway, scurry
              up and down utility poles, those
branchless trees strung together
                with wire. My guess, these impish
creatures remind her of her childhood
              in the country, out a dirt road oiled
every summer to keep down the dust.
            I venture her brothers hunted
those tail-twitchers for the sweetbreads,
              which, when I discovered what they were,
made me squeamish. I'm only one
                generation from poor farmers, families
with a dozen children to dig weeds
                between rows of corn and beans,
to preserve apples and tomatoes,
                to slaughter pigs and cows, to gather
eggs before predators steal them all.
            Even I have loved the owls and whip-
poorwills singing their somber songs.
            I sing a somber song, too. My grandmother
wants iceberg lettuce. She's been told
              leafy greens are good for her blood,
which runs thin, as though she were
              a stretch of land with water slipping
through the hills—crayfish, silversides,
              water striders. She wants chocolate,
something sweet, something the color
              of the richest earth. She's never had

such a sweet tooth before. It must be
            her way of feeding the disease that
empties her body. Soap, butter,
                    mayonnaise. Next week, her needs
will change. So will mine. And if we could
            find a way to live forever, we'd make a list,
mark off every item as we find them.

Afternoon Meditation

Quiet, I try to listen to air,
track its movement through the house.

The air conditioning exhales
an impossible breath. I try to breathe

out as long as I can, but
my lungs are no match. I could be underwater,

surf spilling over as though
it could overtake the continent, heave

itself above every hill,
every tree, every breathing thing. Then

the sky, how easily it moves,
clouds and thunder and lightning. But now,

it hushes. Someone across
the street bounces a basketball, a hollow

echo within a globe. Seismic
waves, the earth nervous in its thin skin.

My sister and I used to play
H-O-R-S-E, a plywood backboard U bolted

to an old antenna truss,
the court a patch of red clay earth. It could

have been the stuff of creation,
this tough soil ceramic under the sun,

malleable after a storm.
Both of my hands start tingling as though

I've been digging through
poison ivy. I've been told that if my right palm

itches, I will meet someone.
If the left, I will receive money. If I could

see the future, I wouldn't
need my grandmother's wisdom. There's

been a breeze all summer,
sometimes so slight only the spiderweb

at the corner of the house
is moved. Hours pass, then years. Sometimes,

I imagine dust as atoms,
that I can see the particles come together

to make everything. My
breathing stirs the star stuff left to settle

in corners, on lampshades,
down the length of curtains. I should

challenge my sister to
another game. I should be happy

with these meager things.

Astigmatism

The aurora in my closed eyes must mean
                                    something, a symbol
for the way the mind works, or for the last
                                    few marbles still rolling
around. Those purples and oranges, reds
                                    and blues, squiggles
and Rorschach blotches in my own private
                                    sky. It's getting cloudy,
and the wanderlust gland in my brain
                                    has altered my chemical
imbalance just enough to make me want
                                    to drive north as far
as a four-door sedan can go, find a way
                                    to cross borders,
undetected. The sun doesn't dance
                                    where I live, near
the confluence of two muddy rivers,
                                    under the haloes
of streetlights. Or kaleidoscope, colors
                                    broken and trapped,
the retina emprismed. I want to see
                                    everything clearer,
a bolt of lightning stopped mid-shock,
                                    hanging in the sky,
Zeus's hand somewhere above the clouds.
                                    I want to see those
great sheets of sunlight laid out upon
                                    the flattest plains,
spill over into canyons, break into sparks
                                    across the ocean.
I shouldn't have said *emprismed*. There's
                                    no such word, and
it sounds as though someone could halt
                                    a proton, hold it

captive. I don't suppose I've ever really
                              believed in any
of those gods, none of those starlings of light.
                    They have to be
described as a vision, a signal to photosensitive
                              cells, interpreted
as something so astonishing it leaves me
                              without explanation.

All I Talk About Is the Weather

It rained last night, fifteen minutes
            after I crossed the threshold, which is
something I seem to be doing all the time.

For instance, the weather. I've reached
            the age when my body predicts
precipitation. Except now, a failure

in my bones. Lately, I've been keeping
            an eye on the ceiling, that shadow
spot above the bed where storms force

their way in. I've tried to fix the problem
            twice. I start watching that Edward
G. Robinson movie, *Our Vines Have Tender*

Grapes, that scene where the two kids
            play "boat" in a tin bathtub, end up
swept away by flood waters, saved

when stopped by a bridge. I always get
            teary-eyed when Robinson scolds
then grabs his daughter tight. I blame it

on a lack of affection, the past untouched.
            The street out front fills with runoff.
I wonder why no one makes paper boats

anymore. Surely, the streams that edge
            and cut through town begin to rush.
Years ago, my grandfather left a few catfish

in a cage tied off in Standing Stone
            Creek. Crawdads found them and
tore them apart, trapped, as they were,

vulnerable to the hunger of others. I've heard
          Robinson named already accused people
as communists to try to save his own career.

I wonder if his father ever hugged him as fiercely
          as he did Margaret O'Brien in that movie.
I can't say I know what that feels like.

Storm upon Us

Almost two in the morning, the singing starts,
first a choir of rain, then an aria of thunder.
                      Imagination kicks up with dust, the first drops

disturbing the soil, the road hissing to surrender
its pent-up heat. The birds that sing to sunlight
                      are hidden, silent under leaves that dance with

the storm. Nights like this were my childhood
reward for oven-baked days of summer,
                      the sheet metal roof of the porch a drum

in the twilight. I haven't played piano in years,
my fingers too forgetful for the compositions
                      of Debussy, Bach, Clementi, Mendelssohn's

"Song without Words" in F sharp minor, one of my
favorite keys for empty hours. I forget which
                      opus this is, the one with little variation

in rainfall, so steady I should be lulled to sleep,
I should be flying in a dream. But nothing
                      attempts flight tonight, no katydid or cicada,

no killdeer, no bat. I know people in other
towns, other cities are out protesting
                      every brutality. The only support I can

give them is sleeplessness, my hopes
they will change the world. In the street,
                      puddles ripple under streetlights, shaking

the way stereo speakers do when filled
with music, the way my heart trembles
                      with treble and bass. Thunder again, the house

shivers. I feel it in my bones, *prestissimo*
at first, then *allegro*, then *larghetto* lingering,
the voices of people gathered in groups so large
they could push back the ocean. If I listen
closely, I might be able to understand all
those words, a downpour, a torrent, a flood.

Another Day of Rain

How can there be anything left to say
about rain? But here it is, dancing
on tree leaves, kissing the long blades

      of grass. Today, there's just no making up
      my mind, one minute cloudburst, the next

a mist that hovers directionless
all afternoon. Coffins have been seen
floating through streets in Louisiana,

      exhumation by flood, bodies adrift
      in the world, the waters of Lethe

or Styx rising to gather all our souls.
In India falls a blood rain that runs
through the streets. You'd think it

      a curse, or a slaughterhouse of the gods,
      all those mythological creatures

skinned and dressed for allegorical tables:
hunger and wanting, gluttony and haunting.
Which is what clouds do all day,

      their hazy bodies halfway between
      earth and elsewhere. Sometimes frogs

fall from the sky. I don't know how
they survive impact, dropped
from those lofty updrafts onto houses,

      into trees, through all those busy streets.
      It is hard not to believe we are

being punished. I know I have been
unkind. How about you? There are those
who remember a gel from an unheavenly

sky, something that brought sickness.
It must have been a sight, people

stepping out onto porches, stopping
their cars to see this goo shimmy down
leaves, down windshields, down stems

of plants barely able to support viscous
matter. What mystery falls upon us?

We are beatified, beautiful
in the rain. No matter
how hard we fall.

Learning to Play Piano

Keyboard in the corner, it's been years
since I plunked out a tune, since I juried
      with Bach and Clementi. I just watched
Casablanca, and I want to play it again.

But all I have is clutter and dust,
old photos and letters and failed artwork
      on the music rack, socks on the speaker,
pens and receipts on the keys. Middle C

my guide, I've learned how to separate
my life, practice counterpoint and
      dissonance. To be honest, I never had
much talent, fingers too clumsy. Piano

lessons with Mrs. Bennett, her family
clattered and slammed while I practiced
      my way through scales and levels.
On Grand Cayman Island, I sat at a piano

bar sipping amaretto while the player
sang through songs older than me, maybe
      older than her, too. I might have had
a few too many, and I might have tried

to sing along, the ocean right outside
doing its best to join right in, hammering
      at the shore, A flat, F sharp, minor third.
Later, I sat in the surf while a couple

made love a hundred yards away. Well,
if I'm honest with myself, it was just sex,
      and I should have gone inside and left them
to seashells and the sound of steel drums.

And, right now, more than anything, I want
to be back on that beach. I want to show
     my lover how the stars skip across the ocean
like stones tossed across a pond. I want to

kiss and converge, dig my hands into the sand.
The fingers must curl, the fingertips a delicate
     touch, a concerto drifting in the breeze, the lights
of ships, unmoored as lost souls looking for Heaven.

After Considering Not Planting a Garden

    Clouds clear, I watch the mail carrier leave
something in the box, probably junk, nothing,

        that is, to keep me from sweating over these
tomato plants I should have put in the ground

            weeks ago. My father may have taught me
how far apart the plants should be spaced,

                but my grandmother told me a little sweat
on the leaves is what makes them grow.

    Her neighbor used to spit on flowers
to assure a good bloom. A couple years ago,

        the tomatoes ripened so fast, there was
no keeping up. No matter how many were

            eaten or given away or put up in jars,
there were always more and more and

                more. Some went bad waiting their turn
on the counter, mush to the touch, a white mold

    around the stem. Gnats, or fruit flies, or
whatever-those-hovering-specks-might-be

        linger for days. I don't expect much from
these vines. It's late in the growing season,

            and the weather goes from flood to drought.
A fool, I will check tomorrow for the slightest

                growth, the subtlest sign of change.
It always seems the weeds grow faster,

    the rubbery stems of purslane, the tangles
of ground ivy, the choking stems of bindweed.

    I wanted zucchini, jalapeños, pole beans, cucumbers. I remember walking the rows

        of corn my father had to lift when a storm made them bow to their gods of wind

        and rain. I remember pulling back tough hulls to check the kernels, snapping off the good ears.

    The buttery feast. I can't predict the bloom, or the setting on of fruit. There may be

        aphids and cutworms, whiteflies, wilt, and rot. There may be days so hot, the body will feel

        like fire, skin ripening in the afternoon sun.

Father's Day

Keeping the Sabbath holy is a chore,
      a matter of tending the lawn.
My grandfather would never have been
seen working on the day of the Lord,
even if the Lord weren't looking.

I never understood why my grandmother
      spent the day peeling potatoes,
browning pork chops, simmering peas and
corn, baking apple and cherry pies as the
afternoon buzzed with four-cycle engines.

There's no wind, and neighbors don't
      even notice as I oversee their toils
like an unseen father. I assume
it is a father's job to criticize my
every move. I mean *our*. *Our*

every move. My father has always been
      a glass maker, and I am a man of glass
marred by bubbles and flaws. We
never went to church, never
populated pews, because my father

wanted me to figure it out for myself. So
      I spent Sundays walking the creek bed,
a stream trickling through mudstone
and sandstone. I would draw my fingers
through red clay, rub it on scratches,

on boils of poison ivy. I felt better
      wearing the earth like this. The clay
dried to dust on my skin. I am not ashes
yet. Probably never will be. After all,
I am glass, a carafe, a window, a jar

filled with heirloom tomatoes.
     As a boy, I used to find marbles
as I dug through the yard, left there
by children who are quite likely
ashes today. The grass will grow

with or without a god. When
     this world ends in fire, and it will,
the day won't matter, the time, all of us
melted, fused, twisted into shapes so fragile
we could crack. We could shatter.

Heritage

Trying to fall asleep all night, it's three in the morning
            as a car passes, radio so loud I swear

the DJ is standing right outside my bedroom window.
            It's not a quick pass. The driver is

deliberately slow, the way I was, at the wheel of
            my father's green pickup. I couldn't

have been more than fourteen years in this world,
            sure I was going out by steering off

the dirt road, careening a hundred feet into the ravine,
            taking some of the second-growth

trees on the way down. I wonder what makes this
            driver passing through this neighbor-

hood so nervous. What makes this driver tremble
            with the decibels of another human

voice, the treble and bass of stock music. Even the walls
            of the house quake, as though

the earth were trembling, trying to create a new rift
            beneath what I thought was safe.

But where did I ever get the idea this world was safe?
            These days, I am a nocturnal creature

moving carefully through the dark, holding still
            as predators draw near. As I do

now, catch my breath before it escapes, then look
            at the clock to see numbers measure

their moments. This moment. A few more hours,
            the sun will take a few steps

into the yard, lean against the apple trees. I made it
down the hill all those years ago,

pumping the brakes, steering close to the ditch and
windswept thistle. My father

had to get out to open the gate to leave his father's
land, where we'd work the last

few weeks of summer for firewood, for something
we could burn.

Maternal

My mother stops by, her bright blue car
        blocking me in. She has another trinket
she thinks I will like, which I will add to
        the roomful of trinkets she's already
given me. She puts the window down,
        doesn't cut the motor, hands over this
new treasure. I say something witty,
        I think. She always laughs, my best
audience, and I've never been that funny.
        Well, no, I take that back. One winter,
walking a snowy, untraveled road, I ran
        up behind my mother to stuff a snowball
down her coat, but I slipped and fell and
        somehow hit myself in the face instead.
Low comedy, slapstick, I know, a Three
        Stooges moment, minus two. And, if
I remember correctly, the sky was just
        the right tone to make the snow look
that color of blue you only see late
        afternoon when the year starts anew.
My mother tells me I have her father's
        eyes, that same cold hue. He's been dead
for twenty years. I was a pall bearer,
        which I hate to remember, sunlight
squeezing through the trees, sky pulled
        flat above. I remember an indigo bunting
almost hidden in dull shadows at the edge
        of the cemetery, a smidge of lazuli in
the undergrowth. It's a cruel joke, finger
        poke to the eyes, hammer to the head.
I never ask my mother if she misses him,
        the man who taught her to drive, the man
whose favorite color still hangs over the clouds
        like a watchful god. But down here on earth,
a little iridescence, barely visible.

Black-and-White Photos

Old pictures, childhood in gray. Easy to believe the world is colorless,
                        just patterns of shadow and light.
If I could capture an EVP of the past, my voice might come through
                        the static of all those years
in playback. I wouldn't listen, anyway. I don't set up cameras
                        to record dust in empty spaces.
The last thing I need to see is draft and drift, mist and mirage. Funny
                        how yesterday is full of ghosts.
In this photo, I am a pale presence holding the pallid swaddling
                        of my sister. Neither of us
old enough to remember the colors of the world. Outside this image
                        must be a cross-hatching
of darkness and illumination. Doesn't it figure? The river ashen.
                        The trees a flutter of smoke.
Somehow, the clouds never change, as in the picture of my father
                        holding me off the chalky sand
at a beach in North Carolina, my hands over my ears to keep the wind
                        from whispering. You can't see it,
except for those loose strands of hair, swept up, washed out
                        in the bleach of the sun.
I don't remember these apparitions, the barely shaded differences.
                        Everything is a matter of gray tones,
charcoal shadings of opinion. And in this picture, my mother's hair
                        is dark, black dress, white pearls.
She stands apart in all these prints, completely defined, unlike the rest of us,
                        fading in and out of dazzle and glare.

Cutting My Hair

               Five minutes, ten tops,
electric shears trim over my ears, different guides
        for different lengths,
always careful to get the angle that suits my face,
        and I'm done.
I used to pay for the convenience, never sure how
        to describe what I wanted.
It's been this way all my life. The high school
        guidance counselor gave up
on me, called me a daydreamer with too many
        lofty goals—rock star,
movie actor, great American novelist. Instead,
        I got parking lot
attendant, bank courier, English professor, poet.
        Tonight, I add barber
to the list. I rinse my hair in the shower to get rid
        of the strays, streetlights
gone cubist through the patterned window. I wish
        I could have been
an artist like my great grandmother who loved
        painting Native American
portraits. But her best was an acrylic of an old
        sycamore, bone white
with golden leaves, wings at the end of every
        branch. It looks ready
to fly, ready to find a new life near some other
        wayward river. I think
of it as a portrait of me, an abstraction only
        I can see. I can
hardly believe all the threads of hair, the smallest
        cuts I cast off,
no longer part of me, my own identity in question
        again. Funny how
I said *own*, as though I know what is mine. I keep
        pictures of me

hidden away, such a Dorian Gray thing to do.
        But they are images
of the past, not who I am today. I've heard
        the only constant
is change. And that may be. There's a moth
        on the window,
I swear, like nothing I've ever seen.

Given Warning

Proof of a heart is a pulse, and thunder
in the middle of the night. More precisely,
                tonight, 2:00 a.m., the sky so loud it wakes

everyone in town, shakes windows, boils
in the body. Nerves try to find their places
                all at once, get in each other's way. Even

emergency sirens go off, scream
their alarm at the suddenness. My instincts
                tell me it's the end of the world.

Every little thing is a sign of destruction, but
I am still here, regardless of every prediction.
                The first time I saw fireworks, I sat close

to my father. I held my ears as I leaned
into his side, hoped he could protect me.
                I thought I might explode, catch fire,

and burn. Now, I sit up in bed and count off
seconds before the rush of rain I know
                will follow. It will sound like ocean waves

rolling over the roof, and I will worry
the whole world is under water. Proof
                of life is wakefulness, and there are lights on

throughout the neighborhood, people
questioning their faith as the heavens
                wash away. As a boy, I watched

Standing Stone Creek rise up to the front door.
My father told me not to worry, that
                we'd be all right. Maybe it's still true.

And if the power goes out, if limbs break
loose in the wind, if transformers spark
            and shatter in the storm, I will remember
how we all survived. Proof of lungs
is a breath, birds singing in broken trees,
            dogs barking at something I've yet to see.

Such a Day as Today

        Inordinate, the amount of light,
every shadow staved off, collapsed

into singularities and absence.
The day is so bright I have forgotten

the history that has grown into a tree
beside the house, leaves of storms

and shootings, riots and surrenders.
I just can't face all that injustice.

How can I stop the sun falling
past the horizon? And, yes, I know

I got that all wrong, but it makes
as much sense halting the spin

of the Earth. And completely selfish,
depriving half the world this wonder,

this gleaming, this blazing comprehension.
        No matter how quickly I move,

I can never capture a handful of light,
enough to carry during the longest

night, to let it glow in my palm,
calming, casting out all my fears,

which are many, more than anyone
should ever keep. How bleak it must be

inside the body, especially the heart,
trapped, as it is

quivering, stopping a moment,
shuddering on.

Incident at Night

Voices outside, in the street,
am I the only one who hears them?

Surely, I'm not alone and awake
at 2:00 a.m., the single soul disturbed

by the nearness of strangers
under a streetlight and a light rain.

I've been known to hear voices,
so I have to look out the window

to be sure. This could be a dream,
a wild mistake of imagination.

But no. This is more substantial,
four young men lost in the hours.

I go to the kitchen, drink
a glass of water. The voices are still

there. I usually hear sirens,
train whistles, barge horns, dogs

barking at things never seen.
There are no spirits here to walk

through our houses, to stir the fog,
to pull at our covers just as we thought

we could go to sleep. But there are
other types of haunting, the unchangeable

past. I wish I could say
there's nothing I would change.

It's too easy to lie. I open the front door,
step out, ask the man in front of my house

if he needs help. He says, *Nope*.
And now I am a voice, disembodied

by shadows, drifting
into neighbors' bedrooms.

Two of the men run off
between houses and trees.

The other two squeal tires and speed
toward other streets. I wait until

the rain whispers, *It is safe*, then I walk
into the road, see nothing but curb

and storm drain. Back inside,
the voices in my head tell me

what I should have done, and
what I shouldn't. But that's the past.

And there's a few more hours before
the sun comes up and the clouds fall apart.

Half the Year Gone

Another milestone, halfway through the year,
    the calendar exposes its staples, the only thing
        holding all these days together. There must be

a superstition for just such a day, something
    about the weather, maybe capturing clouds,
        pulling them close to whisper their secrets

of the future. Or do I mean to the future? Yes,
    that. The future is not an ending. As a child,
        I spent summers with my grandparents,

their plot of suburb on a dead-end street.
    Every few days, a car would pull in, turn
        around in the driveway, leave by the only

path we had to find the rest of the world.
    There was a hickory tree that shaded the end
        of the pavement, every leaf gone gold in autumn.

My grandfather has been dead twenty years.
    There are those who believe this was not his end.
        My grandmother is one of them. Years ago,

I headed east on US 50, just to get away
    from everyone and everything I knew. The road
        ends at a sand dune in Delaware, horseshoe crabs

all over the beach, the Atlantic pounding
    the shoreline, the way it did before anyone
        ever dreamed of gods. Or did Tyrannosaurs

pray to a higher power that didn't survive
    the Cretaceous? Who do I think I'm kidding?
        Those little arms were never meant for prayer.

And the only god dinosaurs knew was a burning
rock from space. But the smallest mammals
survived. They had another deity, one that

burrowed into the soil where roots and beetles
are manna. I'll bet they sang in those underground
chambers. How intricate those unilluminated cathedrals.

Even If It Takes All Night

You'd think nightfall enough
to lull, but the streetlight flares up
at the foot of the bed, burns incessantly.
Some parts of the world fall deeper
into their shadows, and some
shape themselves into creatures
you cannot name. I cannot name
all the reasons why I am unable
to remember my dreams. I turn
the television on again, middle
of the night, just so I'm not alone
in this wakefulness. How many suffer
as I lie here? How many have no home?
I don't even know what I would do.
Would I lean into the warmth
of a brick wall? Would I find comfort
in sheets of newsprint? Would I
steal what I need? Would I beg?
For money? For forgiveness?
For the sound of a stream whispering
over stones throughout the night?
Damn the questions. They pound
at the door, a mob, a riot to drag me
into the streets. Drag me out of my days-
old sheets, throw me in with the laundry.
The whole world's gone stale and fitful,
and I've got a fistful of blanket
tucked in at my side while a movie
flickers, or the news wavers down
the walls. And the lottery picks
have been announced, but I don't have
a ticket. If I'd won, I might've built
houses for the homeless, but now
I'll never know. I'm guilty either way.

Then the sun grays the morning sky
as I close my eyes. Today, there's no right
way to begin, not while the curtains catch
their fair share of dust. Not even prayers
                              would help.

Mapping Stars in City Light

Sirius, the dog star, and Procyon, the little dog,
    I'm in the spill of streetlight

trying to find the brightest stars. Really,
    I should know better, here

in the midst of town where the aura of buildings
    and roadways is stronger

than constellations. Growing up in the country,
    I could see every pinpoint

in the sky, the dancing arm of the galaxy aglow
    across the night. Arcturus,

bear watcher, in the last stages of its life, and
    Vega, the vulture, there are

so many animals in the sky, so many dead heroes
    to keep them company.

I've often dreamed myself among them, a few
    barely blinking lights

in a cluster somewhere near Orion's heel,
    which is called Rigel,

the place where Scorpio stung him in fiercest
    battle. But I've done

my research—Orion was a giant and the worst
    sort of man, the kind

we should all reach up and tear from the sky,
    all those stars falling

in fire upon the world. Canopus is a supergiant,
    and Capella is actually

four stars. I have a hard time orienting myself at this
    confluence of rivers bordering

town, the way they snake and change direction.
    Betelgeuse is a lion

waiting on the other shore, and Achernar is the end
    of this river, which is an ocean,

which is another place too wide to see all at once,
    at least from here. Eventually,

I will go back inside to lamplight, watch a movie
    I've seen a dozen times

before, maybe something science fiction.
    Something that allows me

to weave in and out of stars, and all the fabled
    creatures that live among them.

Spending the Night Alone

    Lured by light,
I could spend all evening
on this porch, a moth
looking for guidance
where there's none to be had.

    The street glows
with its electric stars,
and the creatures that sing
through dusk continue unaware
I'm listening.

    Summer has waited
so long to rise with the sun.
I know cicadas ready themselves
underground near the roots
of trees, their bodies

    rearranging
for the mechanics of flight.
I've never had that dream,
the body overwhelmed
with magic, lifted

    to the clouds.
I've never dreamt of wings.
But now I wonder if
they would blur
like a hummingbird,

    or plank on currents
as a frigate bird. Would physics
tell me I'm a bumblebee,
that I shouldn't be able
to fly? Would I trade my voice

      for rasp of wing
rubbed against wing?
I could be another myth,
storied a tragic end
by all those jealous mortals

      bound to earth
by their wingless forms.
Across the street,
all kinds of creatures frenzy
near any illumination.

      Sounds of machines
and engines echo through
alleys. There are so many
dialects upon darkness.
Here, my neighbor's air

      conditioner speaks
with a lazy tongue.
But when I was a child
with my window open
to the lingering heat

      of summer's breath,
I listened to the whippoorwill,
its voice untouched
by idiom and accent.
If I had wings, I would be

      a nightbird.
and I would sing to bring
down the stars. One by one,
they would fall. I could
gather them, all unwished.

What Keeps Me Up at Night

There is no recipe, no cutouts or clippings
        my grandmother left in a kitchen drawer,
the occasional hand-written list of items

and directions, her script precise and clear.
        It's midnight, and I hunger for her vegetable
soup—carrots, potatoes, celery. Cabbage

brings it all together. Black pepper
        makes it warm. Tomato juice I put up
last year, the heirlooms of my garden,

leaves residue up the sides of the stewpot.
        A few pats of butter mellow as root, leaf,
legume, and kernel soften in the simmer.

I love the feel of a knife in my hand as I slice
        and chop, the tap of the blade against
the cutting board. There's no meat in the mix,

in honor of my vegetarian grandmother
        who grew up on a farm where animals were
slaughtered, the brutality that changed her.

Sometimes, when I can't sleep, I light
        the burners and cook my childhood
memories. I remember a dog barking,

a porch light, a bobcat at the edge of the yard
        where forest was a hodgepodge of shadow
and sycamore and moldering leaves.

I remember being told to stay inside.
        I think I sat at the kitchen window all night
to see if some other wild creature might

stalk me. I had a bowl of soup to lean over,
        steam rising around my face. Even now,
I look out my own window as all this

comes to a boil. Nothing moves near.
        Not even a moth to batter itself
upon glass panes. To try to become

one with the light I leave on throughout
        the night. I don't know why I do this.
Maybe the bobcat was just a symbol.

Maybe I'm remembering it all wrong.

Sleepless

Times like this, when I've lost my faith
                         in humanity, I watch zombie movies
to see every stereotype destroyed.

Even heroes fall prey to the hordes.
                         I read somewhere, years ago, that
these undead masses represent

groupthink, conformity resulting
                         in dysfunction. Belief in gods
is a prime example. One summer,

I stayed with my grandmother
                         while my grandfather was out of town.
I lingered late reading a book

adaptation of *Night of the Living*
                         Dead, and when I got to the passage
of an older woman and her grandson

overpowered by walking cadavers,
                         I had to hide the book, still my frantic
heart, a moth crazed with light,

its wings battered and torn. Now
                         that I know better, I still don't sleep
well. I get up throughout the night,

go to every window, make sure
                         the street is empty. Stripping off
the skin of superstition is torture.

I was born to believe there was
                         a Heaven, born to know there is
a Hell. I fell asleep to the songs

of mourning doves and whippoorwills.
                              Now, I lie awake listening to the whispers
of distant traffic, to the divination of trains,

to the terror of sirens ripping through
                                  shadows to find my door. Where I stand
sometimes in readiness, sometimes with

neediness. If the crickets go quiet, I know
                              something is close. It could be someone
who needs what I no longer have to give.

The Light at Night

Home late, my love already asleep
        on the other side of town. Across the street,
a parked car in the school lot, headlights
        shine through my bedroom window.
The streetlight, yes, I get. That's a constant
        intrusion, a sense of comfort when I wake
in darkness to see that bit of radiance
        at the foot of the bed. The full moon, too,
every month a clock in the heavens

        counting minutes across the floor.
Sometimes, I count the hours. But this car,
        can't they tell their light is unwanted,
that it cuts through the night I love?
        I've been told I'm difficult to live with.
I don't deny it. I rarely check the time

        after lovemaking. I have greater concerns.
Sometimes, a police car sits hidden
        in the shadows of the park to catch people
like me speeding through town, people like me
        so full of something akin to happiness.
Happy with fiery affection, yes, but something else.

        Another ten minutes, then I'll go out
and ask whoever's sitting in that car
        to please cut the halogens aimed at my room.
Maybe they have a short temper. Maybe
        they have a gun or a knife. And me
in whatever clothes I manage to pull on

> before this confrontation. I must be a fool.
Maybe they are a lover, too. Maybe spent.
> Maybe spurned. And this little bit of light

is all they have to remind them there is
> always something in those microscopic
moments before dawn, something

> only a matter of a few feet in front of the car.
Something, maybe just a moth dancing
> in rapture, in light, before us.

Emblematic

A dragonfly perches on a trumpet vine
blossom. I've been trying to untangle
                    this invasive plant from the fence. It
keeps reminding me that there are
such things as a fresh start, a new
                    beginning. The dragonfly doesn't
know it, but it is the embodiment of
joy. My grandfather dug a pond on
                    his farm. He knew there would be
cattails, water lilies, and frogs, which
are bringers of rain. Something in
                    their songs calls to the sky in a way
my voice cannot. I don't know how
many birds sing on my backyard fence
                    above the floss flower, a little wild
left untouched in my life. I grew up
beside a dirt road where daisies and
                    dewberries crowded for sunlight,
where I caught tadpoles in tire ruts,
where I captured a whiptail lizard
                    sunning itself on sandstone. Lizards
are symbols of resurrection, which
implies faith. When my grandfather
                    was dying, he believed things he'd
never believed before. A minister
prayed over him, a blackbird guarding
                    its treasure. I've heard crows will
steal objects that glint in sunlight,
though this is probably a myth.
                    This is just something I love to think
is true. I've never been fast enough,
or I've never been diaphanous enough
                    to catch a dragonfly, which I just

learned cannot walk, if I trust what I
read. So joy must be that moment a
                    predator draws near, and being able
to see everything at once, coming back
to the same spot, overly sure there is
                    some way to careen out of reach.

Funeral Planning

Tempers flare, burst forth from the sun.
My grandmother calls today to tell me
      she's mad at my aunt, her daughter
who keeps her scheduled, her doctor
appointments marked on a calendar.
      I still don't understand what happened.
The little I know is she wants to cancel all
her medical consultations, and my aunt
      responds that she's not taking her
anywhere ever again. They could be
children on the playground, clinging
      to monkey bars and jungle gym,
the hottest hour of the hottest day
of the year. I want to be angry,
      but all I can do is laugh and think
about the blazing stars that begin
to bloom along my driveway, one of
      the few flowers that blossoms top down,
like sparklers in the pinch of children's fingers,
toddlers giggling through another long evening.
      Autumn will be too soon upon us, and
everyone will blush as we remember
our foolishness. My grandmother hates
      all the seasons anymore. I think it has
to do with obvious changes, robins
to whippoorwills, cicadas to crickets,
      crows to juncos, whiteflies to gnats.
I've never really thought about
the shreds and threads at the end
      of life. Yesterday, I received a notice
for a pre-planning seminar from a local
funeral home. I've fallen under the delusion
      that I can last as long as the sun, halfway

through its mortality. It will give up the ghost
by expanding, going red giant, then tearing
             itself apart. This is how I want to go,
captivating everyone with all that light.

Foresight

Every spring,
my grandfather burned
a pasture,

scorched and blackened
thistle and fleabane right
to the tree line

where mice
and bees escaped
the slow advance

of low flames.
It was the end of the world
in increments,

the ragged
approach of a god's wrath.
But which god

I couldn't say.
The god of fescue, the god
of meadows,

the god of grazing?
All season long, resurrection
broke out

all over the field.
Later, cattle survived on this
manna, the small herd

my grandfather kept,
some for milk, some for meat.
I never saw

the slaughter,
the sacrifice, except when
squirrel hunting,

my father
made me help him
skin the creatures,

their gray pelts
limp on the ground. But that was
autumn, after

the garden's
last harvest, tomato vines
brittle as bones,

corn stalks cackling
with a touch of wind. Every day,
a little closer to firelight

and superstition,
I thought this was how
witches were born,

from the uncut
fields of corn, a spell
cast under

a lagging moon,
the shadows of papery leaves.
I thought

bad luck
was a matter of misreading signs,
first frost

six months
from first thunderstorm.
Wisdom and witchery

were the same,
honey for bee sting,
vinegar for wasp,

grab your earlobe
to stop the pain of a burn.
I watched

my grandfather
beat the fire out with a shovel,
throw buckets of water

to drown the embers.
I watched smoke rise
through branches

and leaves.
There was nothing on earth
could catch it.

By Another Name

Corvus brachyrhynchos is Latin
for common crow, which I thought was my spirit
animal, when I thought I had
a spirit. *Anima mea* is Latin for soul. I have a sense
of secret identities, pseudonyms,
aliases, AKAs. My mother studied Latin in high school
with practical thoughts of becoming
a nurse, but that's part of an unresolved past.
The past, which is the home
of the dead. Like a name no longer used, my mother's
discarded in marriage.
What I call mourning dove, my grandmother calls
rain crow. What I call
fetters, so many call love. Every living thing has
another name, a world
out of reach, unspoken. Coptic, Sanskrit, Akkadian.
Sometimes, I feel my shadow
is a remnant, a wordless tongue, listless lips.
I dream of the heavens,
caelum, which is also a constellation in the southern
sky, a chisel to penetrate
the darkness. My grandfather used a chisel to cut
stone into blocks, dragged
by oxen, foundation for his home, *domum*,
domicile, dwelling. I could
have names falling from me, an oak late in autumn
shrugging off its leaves,
even in winter, the wind speaking lost syllables
through branches. And there
should be crows, yes, crows, raucous and rasping,
complaining that this world
is not enough, no language so poetic it can build
a house from light and rain.

Ever Changing

The cats have fleas again, jump
on counters and bookshelves
           to avoid the plague. I just read that

someone in California contracted
an ancient disease, probably

in the usual manner, vermin,
rodents, parasites. When I was
           a child, my father told me the plague

killed everybody, so I believed
we had to re-evolve. We had to

crawl out of the slime, repeat
all the same mistakes. It was too
           late when I realized my father

was prone to exaggeration, that close
cousin to deception. As a result,

I still don't know how to recognize
the truth. First, I hear there's
           an insect apocalypse, almost

half of all bugs face extinction.
Then, I'm reassured that they'll

outlast everyone and everything.
And I wonder if it's my fault
           there were fewer fireflies

to make a galaxy in my back yard,
if I should take the blame for

the absence of honeybees
among apple blossoms. And I have
           to stop talking about the past.

One of the cats slipped away last week.
I swear I see its ghost every now

and then in my peripheral vision.
Which is probably where all of reality
            exists, not in front, but off to the side.

The television flickers to my left,
and a window darkens to my right.

Television means distant sight,
as though some small part of the future
            could come into view and change

the way I walk around town, barely
glancing through the windows

of restaurants, theaters, banks
and offices, the sun losing its fight
            with the heavens. If I lose my sight

and must relearn the world, I've already counted
the steps it takes to make my way through this world.

Desire

Feral felines have their kittens hidden
under the neighbor's ramshackle shed,

in the thicket of untrimmed berry vines.
They've been thinning out the arias

of songbirds. I know who I love. I fear
when birds are gone, I will no longer

desire updrafts and altitude. What happens
to predators when there is nothing to hunt?

Haunches shift in overgrown weeds.
Eyes focus, unblinking. My lover falls

victim to Eros, that vengeful god, who unfurls
his wings to reveal himself irresistible.

How softly the goddess purrs. Her children
suckle, but crave the blood. The end

must be like this, with gods eating grapes and
pomegranates, sitting near a waterfall,

where all else goes unheard. My love
sleeps beside me. This is as close as we get

to safe. My eyes are hunters. A bird
I can't identify arrows and feathers the sky.

I am a wasted target. Another bird sings.
I should be able to name it, but I can't.

I can't even imagine the words. A cat stalks,
climbs, claws. I must be a long-bodied

carnivore, hungry for all those
winged creatures, ravenous for angels.

I know how swift they can be.

Entomology

Fireflies are sparse tonight, only two
or three in these vast hours, when
                there should be enough to confound
the heavens. I've heard they are
dying off, and since I'm far from
                the twilight of childhood, I must be
dying off, too. If I had named them,
I wouldn't have used *fire* or *lightning*.
                I would have called them *starflies*
or *nova bugs*. But perhaps that's
too grand for something so brief.
                Late spring was like watching the birth
of the universe take place in the yard,
in the trees. A few days ago, I read
                about bombardier beetles. I love
how that resonates. *Bombardier,
bombardier, bombardier*, the violent
                opening and closing of the lips,
the explosion of sound. It seems
preposterous an insect should
                have a chemistry set inside its body,
spray a burning liquid toward whatever
it fears. How many years of evolution
                does it take to make such a creature?
For instance, the assassin bug, a name
that makes me think of history,
                politics, Macbeth, the way this insect
stabs its victim repeatedly. When was
the last time I read Macbeth?
                I couldn't say. I don't remember
any mention of arthropods. The witches
around their bubbling cauldron rhyme
                their prophecy, snake and newt,
bat and hellbender. I like to imagine

the fields all around full of bug chatter,
                        casting spells, and *rising, rising*.
I conjure fireflies, living comets,
and me running out to catch them.

Off the Earth

Sassafras comes up from the roots of my neighbor's tree,
        the lawn riddled
with these sucker plants. My neighbor is a ghost now.

        Whoever it is lives
there today, I don't know them. But this tree I know.

        My great grandmother
told me she steeped the root bark for tea, reminiscent
        of root beer, told me

it was good for whatever ailed the body, whatever troubled
        the soul. She also

let dandelions burst across the yard, so she could gather
        the greens for salad.
I've never had her taste for what is wild, a bee to its clover,

        butterfly weed
to its bright spot in the sun. There must be fifty or more

        shoots all spreading
in the shade of these dove-shaped leaves. If I let them,
        they would spread

quick as fire. And the trumpet vine on the fence would
        grab the corner

of the house, overwhelm the walls, the roof, the windows
        and doors. How easily
I could be trapped, a folk story of a man surrounded by vines,

        a desperate voice
drifting out of the tangles to lure people in, who are never

        seen again. I get
down on my knees in the brittle August grasses, a supplicant
        to summer heat,

and I break the sapling stems with my bare hands. I whisper
                    my regrets

to the earth that only wants to offer new growth. Anyone
                            watching might
think I'm praying. But I'm not. My great grandmother

                        may be listening,
her back bent with years of collecting low-growing

                        curatives. Even
the poisonous milkweed feeds a caterpillar, its body
                            filling with flight.

Neighbors

My sister was married in the breezeway
      at the house that was to become mine,
my great grandmother's where she sat
on her glider with daisies in her hair. Her name
was Leafy, a name her mother heard whispered
      in the woods. The preacher next door
conducted the ceremony, but now there's
a young family in his house. They might
as well be ghosts or cryptids, so rarely seen.
      On the other side is a mother and her
forty-something bachelor son, three cars
and a truck on their front lawn. The son
leaves every morning at 4:00 a.m., which
      I only know because I'm still awake.
When the streets go quiet, and storms pass
on to other towns, I cannot stop myself
what-iffing the world. And judging by light
      in a few distant windows, there are others
who do the same. The house behind me
was vacant so long the air went stale
from stillness. I've been told someone
      moved in, but that could be a rumor
meant to allay fears of squatters or addicts,
which is all too common anymore. And
across the street, a woman sits on her porch
      late into the night. I wonder if she knows
I see her. I wonder if she knows I watch her
and her lover come home drunk on the
weekends, stumble through the door.
      My sister and I only see each other twice
a year, during the longest holidays. Her
children are at that age when they try
to forget her. They want to travel other
      streets, sleep in the proximity of
unfamiliar houses and unrelated sidewalks,

which is okay. Tomorrow, I will call
my mother. She will tell me what she
          remembers since last we talked.

Cut Glass Candy Dish

                I live in the house
where my great-grandmother died, where
                        she put a pot of coffee
on the stove and forgot about it, where she
                          grew mint in the shade
at the end of the breezeway just for the scent
                        in summer. Twenty
years and I've never seen her ghost, only
                         reminders, her paring
knife in the utensil drawer, her recipe book
                         written in tidy cursive,
her candy dish, cut glass, probably a flea market
                        or yard sale find.
Twenty years, and just today I miss her.
                        There are no heirlooms
in my family, only cheap hand-me-downs.
                        When I was eight,
or ten, or twelve, I had to wear my cousin's
                        western-style shirts.
He'd outgrown them and the desire to be
                        a cowboy. So I took on
someone else's dreams, someone else's past
                        life in stitch and cloth.
My mother bought me cowboy boots I couldn't
                        wear, high arches,
or some defect of my birth. Which has to have been
                        passed down as well.
My ancestry is a yellowed letter found stuck
                        in the back of a drawer,
a concern that someone could break into the house
                        and take what they want.
My great-grandmother never locked her doors.
                        Two nights ago, I accidentally
left the front door open, slept without a thought
                        about safety. If I dreamed,

I couldn't say. I sleep fitfully, which is something
                I inherited from the women
in my family. A year after I moved in, a young
                girl rang the bell,
asked me where the nice, old lady was. I said,
                I'm sorry. I said,
She's no longer with us. I have no idea
                if she understood.

Impossible Solitude

Proxima Centauri cannot be seen, too faint
                    a star to make itself known to my failing
eyes. I doubt I could find it with the trickery
                    of lenses and magnification. There are days
I can't even find my wallet and keys.
                    I think of the sun as a lonely flame, isolated,
light years from brothers and sisters
                    and distant cousins. Some of my relatives
sling themselves across the continent,
                    inertia pushing us all apart. Some of them
jump oceans, getting father away. I don't
                    know any of their names. They could be
far-flung at the edge of the universe
                    surrounded by dark matter and emptiness.
Sometimes, I think my sister does not exist,
                    a woman of mythology in a pattern of stars,
the feminine form balanced on a tree limb
                    suspended over a stream. A beech tree,
leaves with jagged edges, and she already
                    on her way to the sky. It's August now
and the creek is likely mud and stones
                    and puddles. I also believe my grandfather
never existed, nor his place of birth,
                    his unexamined life, his plot of earth.
Death is like that. The moon turns away
                    when the world is just too much,
taking to seclusion when I am too hostile,
                    too angry, too destructive. One day, I know,
I will learn self-control. Every night to follow
                    will be graced by a full moon,
night after night I tell myself. I promise.

Mythology

Silver poplars, I call them ghost
                trees, so pale
they look as though they move
                between this
world and another. The one in
                my neighbor's
yard is half dead, bare branches
                sticking out, bones
robbed of their flesh, surrounded
                by leaves jangling
in the breeze. My grandfather
                called them silver
maple, but that's an entirely
                different tree,
the kind that only shows their
                otherworldliness
when wind blows off the river,
                through the open
spaces of town. I've always had
                a love/hate
relationship with the past, a cruel
                compassion for
all the people I've left behind.
                Anyone who
has ever had to abandon a lover,
                drive through
the desert to forget their name,
                these are the people
who know. Some day soon, I have
                to prune saplings
from the chain link fence just to
                slow the natural
world from taking over. Entropy
                already climbs

in morning glory and rust. When
                        this ghost is gone,
I will miss it, whatever name I give.
                        Among all
the backyard trees, the verdant
                        suncatchers,
this pale thing stands alone. I know
                        only one tree
more inconsolable, the weeping
                        willow by the river
where my uncle lived until his heart
                        stopped while
he was standing beneath its
                        despondent
limbs, his wife finding him there,
                        a few discarded
leaves fallen. I could name hundreds
                        of trees for
the hundreds of ways they change
                        in this life.
Even the gods used to transform
                        people as verdure.
I wonder who must have been
                        punished and left
here with sallow foliage. I know
                        which tree grows
in my bones, ready for its leaves.

Pandemic

My nephew tags everyone, yells *you're it*
as he touches each of us, then runs away.
        This is last year,
or five years ago or ten. Time floods and washes away.
Today, my family is distant, an hour's drive or more,
        at the very least.
My sister orders everything online, never leaves
the house, her husband essential but working
        from home.
I've always been terrified of people. If someone
knocks on my door, I freeze and wait for them to leave.
        This could be the plague
of Athens, or Antonine, or Cyprian, or Justinian.
This could be Black Death or Yellow Fever.
        This could be "The Mask
of the Red Death," which I just read again, each word,
each letter infectious. Every little ache in the body
        becomes a symptom:
heartburn, foot cramp, hangnail, bit lip.
How old is my nephew now? Last week
        he was eight.
This week he's eighteen. I can keep my distance.
I can stay away. I can sit alone for years.
        Given enough time,
I can disappear. Even the neighbors will wonder
if I'm still alive. When I emerge, I will be *it*.
        I will start all over again,
but stronger, harder to fight off,
lingering imperceptibly on the breath.

Rain Crow

Supposedly, mourning doves mate for life,
        which means their instinct for courtship rituals
is used only once. After that, there is only nesting

or grief. Grief is an instinct, almost a punishment
        for loving what we cannot hold onto, no matter
how hard we try. I don't mean to question

the claims of ornithologists with the word
        supposedly. I believe the science and observation.
Bald eagles and mute swans also practice

monogamy. The whooping crane, too.
        And there are others that show their devotion
in feathers and flight, migration and molt.

This morning, one dove calls for rain,
        which is what my grandmother taught me,
to believe in superstition, explanations

of the world through fear and fantasy. Now
        that I am older, I feel the approach of clouds.
Why don't I sing? Why don't I go to the door

and croon for the coming storm? *Plaintive*.
        That's another word. Especially when I turn
the television on in another room to keep

the house from feeling lonely. I'd be lying
        if I said the house was not a symbol for me.
Prevarication runs in my veins. And the dove

is purported to be a symbol for peace,
        but I haven't seen much of that around here
lately. Though I must admit the hour is still.

Barometric pressure drops too slowly for a storm.
    Maybe a light rain or drizzle, just enough to keep me indoors, haunting every room. I wouldn't normally

think myself a ghost, but this trill and coo is spiritual.
    No wonder the gods choose birds as vessels.
My favorite dream is the one in which I can fly.

Where There is Forgiveness

I suppose because it's Sunday
        and the air is quiet with penitence,
I think of my spotty history
        with church. My lover believes

in God, all the rigmarole of kneeling,
        praying, striving for Heaven.
I've never been one for unquestioned faith,
        what with a preacher who tells me

I am damned, and me in a pew
        with my hands clasped. The sun smears
stained-glass colors upon my hand,
        down my leg. But this is all

scientific, fusion, photon,
        transpiration. Transubstantiation,
my lover tells me, is a miracle,
        the Light of the Lord taken

into the body where the soul
        stays out of sight. The deepest pit
of the ocean seems a great place
        to hide, and must be the origin

of all those washed-up, unidentified
        creatures, those globsters, masses of flesh
carried on the foaming sea, moved
        by waves rearranging the shore.

They are mysterious, these cryptids,
        revealed only in death. It's natural,
isn't it, to wonder what else might be
        hidden? Sunlight cannot penetrate

the fathoms where beasts and beings
        make themselves luminous.
If they wandered through our homes,
        drifted in and out of doors,

we would call them spirits. Some might
        consider them angels. I am not
one of them, neither prophet nor apparition.
        If I've learned anything from Dante,

I know that who we love can find us.
        I've heard expiation is more
than making amends. I've heard
        you have to mean it.

Those Who Stay Behind

       Finally, a phoebe shows up
on my backyard fence. With a name
       like that, I imagine veils
and silk feathers, lustrous as mother-
       of-pearl. The second
breeding season is over, two clutches,
       sixteen days to hatchlings,
sixteen more to fledge. *Dun*, yes,
       that's a good word
for her. *Dun*. I don't know what
       makes me think this bird
is female. Possibly a newly discovered
       freedom. Possibly
a wild precision for catching insects
       mid-flight. There's a look
about this bird I attribute to my mother.
       Her song I attribute to
a young woman transformed by an
       unruly god. Some of
those gods are here now. I've been
       trying to discourage them
gathering near the spearmint at the end
       of my driveway.
They wait for me to come home every
       night. Above us,
a turkey vulture skims the sky, which
       I've always thought
meant death was near. But, today,
       flight is simply
an expression of joy, tempting the pallid
       clouds to reach down,
join the exaltation. When my parents
       divorced, my mother
became a different person, which made me
       different, too. Migration

will begin soon, but some birds will remain,
        survive on whatever's left
behind. And I've left so much behind.
        Perhaps there's something
supernatural hiding among the unripe apples,
        and maybe that's why
the phoebe is here. Soon, the world will
        be left to cardinal,
jay, and crow. Soon, even without leaves,
        trees will lean
into the sun, nostalgic, unsettled.

Apocalypse

Hot air moves to find some comfort, a breeze
                         that could cause a blaze.
The first cicada of the season scrapes its ungodly
                         voice like a flint in the
water maple. I expect the top of the tree to
                         burst into flames. As a
teenager, it was my job to burn the trash in
                         a fifty-gallon metal drum,
match to paper, flare to rubbish. I loved
                         watching those fingers
of fire reach up, demons trying to escape the
                         bonds of Hell. Cicadas
had risen again, seventeen years beneath
                         the soil, a resurrection
of sorts, a plague of noise and glassy wings.
                         One flew into my sister's
hair, her panic stilled as I pinched those wings,
                         carried that insect devil
to the inferno and threw it in. I'm not proud of
                         my cruelty. I used to
catch leaf hoppers and millers to throw into
                         spiderwebs, watch their
struggles as spiders tight-wire walked toward
                         them. I've always thought
spiders looked hungry, ravenous, never sated.
                         Perhaps this is the source
of my fear, the hunger of heights, the cravings
                         of crowds, the appetite of
night. The end of the world was so much
                         farther away back then.
I've heard the world will end in fire, the ravings
                         of a Baptist preacher who
only saw damnation for me, which I knew was
                         true. If today is any

indication, it must be true, sunlight spilling itself
             at my feet, and me
just learning how to dance.

Biography

David B. Prather's first collection, *We Were Birds*, was published by Main Street Rag Publishing in 2019. He has another full-length poetry collection, *Shouting at an Empty House*, forthcoming from Sheila-Na-Gig Editions. He served as a juror for Ohio State Poet Laureate Kari Gunter-Seymour's anthology, *I Thought I Heard a Cardinal Sing: Ohio's Appalachian Voices*. He is a past president of West Virginia Writers, Inc., a statewide non-profit organization. He taught English Composition, American Literature, and Creative Writing at West Virginia University at Parkersburg and English Composition at Marietta College in Marietta, Ohio. He also served as poetry editor for *Confluence Literary Journal* and for Tantra Press, and he hosted the Blennerhassett Reading Series. He currently serves as a reader for *Suburbia Journal*. His poetry, essays, and reviews have appeared in many journals, including *Colorado Review, Seneca Review, Prairie Schooner, The American Journal of Poetry, The Literary Review, Poet Lore*, and others. His work has also appeared in many anthologies, including *Voices from the Fierce Intangible World* (from *South Florida Poetry Journal*) and *Endlessly Rocking: Poems in Honor of Walt Whitman's 200th Birthday* (Unbound Content, Englewood, New Jersey). He studied acting at the National Shakespeare Conservatory in New York, and he appeared in a couple of local (West Virginia/Ohio) independent movies. He received his MFA from Warren Wilson College in North Carolina. And he lives in the town where he was born—Parkersburg, West Virginia.

Acknowledgments

All poems were originally published with "Journal Entry:" as the introductory title words and in this or similar form.

Clackamas Literary Review / "Off the Earth"
Crowstep Journal / "Foresight"
Cutleaf Journal / "Mapping Stars in City Light"
Front Range Review / "Maternal"
Hive Avenue Literary Journal / "Another Day of Rain"
In the Midst: A Covid-19 Anthology / "Pandemic"
Jasper's Folly Poetry Journal / "After Considering Not Planting a Garden," and "The Light at Night"
Literary Heist / "Germination"
Lothlorien Poetry Journal / "Storm Upon Us"
The Meadow: Literary and Arts Journal / "Rain Crow"
Muddy River Poetry Review / "Entomology," and "186,000 Miles Per Second"
Psaltery & Lyre / "Apocalypse"
The Raconteur Review / "Lightning," and "Maintenance"
Red Tree Review / "Memorial Day"
Rockvale Review / "A Drop in Barometric Pressure"
Shark Reef / "Even If It Takes All Night"
Sheila-Na-Gig / "Cutting My Hair," and "What Keeps Me Up at Night"
Verse-Virtual / "Black-and-White Photos"

Voice Lux Journal / "All I Talk About is the Weather," and "Desire" *The Wild Word Magazine* / "Those Who Stay Behind"

"What Keeps Me Up at Night" was also published in the anthology, *Sharing This Delicate Bread: Selections from Sheila-Na-Gig* online 2016–2021

Title Index

Numbers

186,000 Miles Per Second 14

A

A Drop in Barometric Pressure 27
After Considering Not Planting a Garden 47
Afternoon Meditation 35
All I Talk About Is the Weather 39
Another Day of Rain 43
Apiary 20
Apocalypse 105
Astigmatism 37

B

Black-and-White Photos 54
By Another Name 83

C

Cut Glass Candy Dish 93
Cutting My Hair 55

D

Dental Work 21
Desire 86

E

Electrical Grid 31
Emblematic 76
Entomology 87
Even If It Takes All Night 64
Ever Changing 84

F

Father's Day 49
Fear of Darkness 12
Foresight 80
Freeze Warning 15
Funeral Planning 78

G

Germination 17
Given Warning 57

H

Half the Year Gone 62
Heritage 51

I

Impossible Solitude 95
Incident at Night 60

L

Learning to Play Piano 45
Lightning 29

M

Maintenance 18
Mapping Stars in City Light 66
Maternal 53
Memorial Day 23
Mythology 96

N
Neighbors 91

O
Off the Earth 89
One Month Until Summer 25

P
Pandemic 98

R
Rain Crow 99

S
Shopping for My Grandmother During a Pandemic 33
Sleepless 72
Spending the Night Alone 68
Storm upon Us 41
Such a Day as Today 59

T
The Light at Night 74
Those Who Stay Behind 103

W
What Keeps Me Up at Night 70
Where There is Forgiveness 101

First Line Index

A

A dragonfly perches on a trumpet vine 76
A dull headache for two days is one of my signs 27
Almost two in the morning, the singing starts 41
Aluminum siding needs painted 18
Another milestone, halfway through the year 62
A skunk has moved into the area, rummaging 25

C

Clouds clear, I watch the mail carrier leave 47
Corvus brachyrhynchos is Latin 83

E

Every spring 80

F

Feral felines have their kittens hidden 86
Finally, a phoebe shows up 103
Fireflies are sparse tonight, only two 87
Five minutes, ten tops 55

H

Home late, my love already asleep 74
Hot air moves to find some comfort, a breeze 105
How can there be anything left to say 43

I

I live in the house 93
Inordinate, the amount of light 59
I suppose because it's Sunday 101
It rained last night, fifteen minutes 39

J

Judging by the clouds this morning, unmoved 29

K

Keeping the Sabbath holy is a chore 49
Keyboard in the corner, it's been years 45

L

Lately, I begin to wonder how long it'll be 12
Lured by light 68

M

My father brings me seeds he ordered from a catalog 17
My mother stops by, her bright blue car 53
My nephew tags everyone, yells you're *it* 98
My sister and I never knew the dead 23
My sister was married in the breezeway 91

O

Old pictures, childhood in gray.
    Easy to believe the world is colorless 54

P

Pigeons perch on power lines for two days 31
Proof of a heart is a pulse, and thunder 57
Proxima Centauri cannot be seen, too faint 95
Purplish blooms, my blazing stars 20

Q
Quiet, I try to listen to air 35

R
Running late again, I meant to be 14

S
Sassafras comes up from the roots of my neighbor's tree 89
She tells me, again, that she won't 33
Silver poplars, I call them ghost 96
Sirius, the dog star, and Procyon, the little dog 66
Sometimes mistaken for a flying insect 21
Supposedly, mourning doves mate for life 99

T
Tempers flare, burst forth from the sun 78
The aurora in my closed eyes must mean 37
The cats have fleas again, jump 84
There is no recipe, no cutouts or clippings 70
Three ghostly figures stand motionless 15
Times like this, when I've lost my faith 72
Trying to fall asleep all night, it's three in the morning 51

V
Voices outside, in the street 60

Y
You'd think nightfall enough 64

www.ingramcontent.com/pod-product-compliance
Lightning Source LLC
Chambersburg PA
CBHW011947150426
43193CB00019B/2927